emotions

Always remember,

problems

are yours...

The material in this book is selected from various talks by Osho
given to a live audience. All of Osho's talks have been published in
full as books, and are also available as original audio recordings.
Audio recordings and the complete text archive can be found via the
online OSHO Library at www.osho.com/library

OSHO is a registered trademark of OSHO International Foundation
www.osho.com/trademarks

OSHO MEDIA INTERNATIONAL
New York • Zurich • Mumbai
an imprint of
OSHO INTERNATIONAL
www.osho.com/oshointernational

Distributed by Publishers Group Worldwide
www.pgw.com

Printed in India by Manipal Technologies Limited, Karnataka

ISBN: 978-1-938755-92-7
Also available as eBook: ISBN: 978-0-88050-778-3

emotions

Freedom from Anger, Jealousy and Fear

contents

medical disclaimer

Any advice or teachings given in this book are not
intended to replace the services of your physician,
psychotherapist, or psychiatrist. Nor is it meant to
provide an alternative to professional medical treatment. This book offers no diagnosis of or treatment
for any specific medical or psychological problems
that you may have. Before you start any intensive
exercises which may be part of some of the meditations, consult your physician.

introduction

The title of this little book might give readers the idea that they have found another "how to" book. Not at all – this book will provide you with a different dimension, where all the questions about "how" are dissolved into a direct perception of your own, hidden reality.

Osho says:

"We reduce everything into a how. There is a great how-to-ism all over the world and every person, particularly the modern contemporary mind, has become a how-to-er: how to do this, how to do that, how to grow rich, how to be successful, how to influence people and win friends, how to meditate, even how to love. The day is not far off when some stupid guy is going to ask how to breathe. It is not a question of how at all. Don't reduce life into technology. Life reduced into technology loses all flavor of joy."

Here you will find insights to unlock your own intuitive understanding of yourself and your inner world.

Some of the ideas you encounter may disturb you, may go against everything you think you already know. Others may fill you with the shock of recognition, as they bring words to a truth that it suddenly feels you have always known.

Whatever the case, relax…give it some time to sink in and watch. Come back to it again and again – and soon you will find new levels of understanding growing between the lines as you come closer and closer to the truth of your own being.

No, this is not a "how to" book. It is a lamp that you can use, no matter who you are, to light the hidden corners of your own unique individuality.

CHAPTER 1

what are emotions?

What are your thoughts except ripples on a lake?

What are your emotions, your moods,
your sentiments?
What is your whole mind? – just a turmoil.
And because of this turmoil you cannot see
your own nature.
You go on missing yourself.
You meet everybody in the world and you never
meet yourself.

—

You are angry, but you cannot remain angry forever.
Even the angriest man laughs sometimes, has to.
It cannot become a permanent state of affairs,
being angry.

Even the saddest man smiles;
and even the man who laughs continuously
sometimes cries and weeps and tears come to his
eyes.
Emotions cannot be permanent.
That's why they are called "emotions"!
The word comes from "motion," movement.
They move; hence, they are emotions.
You continually change from one to another.

This moment you are sad,
that moment you are happy;
this moment you are angry,
that moment you are very compassionate;
this moment you are loving,
another moment full of hatred;
the morning was beautiful,
the evening is ugly. This goes on.

The ordinary commonsense view
is that the heart is the source of emotions like love
or hate or anger. Just as the mind is the source of
conceptual thoughts, the heart is the source of all
that is emotional and sentimental.
That is the commonsense view.

—

We have lived with this traditional division,
that imagination and feeling and emotions
and sentiments are of the heart.

But your heart is just a pumping system.
Everything that you think or imagine or feel
is confined in the mind.
Your mind has seven hundred centers
and they control everything.

—

When a person like Buddha talks about "the heart"
he means the very center of your being.
It is his understanding that your love,
your hate, everything, arises out of your mind.
And I think he is being absolutely scientific;
all psychologists will agree with him.

You can experiment yourself.
You can see from where your anger arises – it is the
mind;
from where your emotions arise – it is the mind.

Mind is a big phenomenon.
It covers conceptual thinking,
it covers your emotional patterns, your sentiments.

—

This has to be understood: emotions are in your head! But consciousness is not in your head. In fact, your head is in your consciousness! Consciousness is vast, infinite.

Emotions, desires, ambitions, are in your head; they will dry up. But even when your head has completely dropped and disappeared into the earth, your consciousness will not disappear. You don't contain the consciousness, the consciousness contains you; it is bigger than you.

—

It is absolutely true.

Your emotions, your sentiments, your thoughts – the whole paraphernalia of the mind – is from the outside, is manipulated by the outside. Scientifically it has become more clear.

But even without scientific investigation the mystics, for thousands of years, have been saying exactly the same thing – that all these things that your mind is filled with are not yours, you are beyond them.

—

You get identified with them,
and that's the only sin.

—

Mind is a division which thinks,
and heart is another division of the same mind which
feels.

Feeling and thinking,
thoughts and emotions...
but witnessing is separate from both.
When you are thinking, the watcher watches... A
thought is passing by, or you are feeling angry – the
witness still watches. An emotion is passing by, just
like clouds pass, and you see them.

You are neither the good nor the bad.
You are neither the pleasant nor the unpleasant.
You are neither the thought nor the emotions.
You are neither the mind nor the heart.

—

Love always makes one nervous

There are reasons why it makes one nervous. It comes from the unconscious, and all your capacities are in the conscious; all your skill, all your knowledge, is in the conscious. Love comes from the unconscious and you don't know how to cope with it, what to do with it, and it is too much.

The unconscious is nine times bigger than the conscious, so whatsoever comes from the unconscious is overwhelming. That's why people are afraid of emotions, feelings. They hold them back, they are afraid they will create chaos.

They do, but chaos is beautiful!
There is a need for order, and there is a need for chaos too. When order is needed use order, use the conscious mind; when chaos is needed use the unconscious, and let chaos be. A whole person, a total person, is one who is capable of using both, who does not allow any interference of the conscious into the unconscious or of the unconscious into the conscious.

We believe in life in its totality:
in its days,
in its nights,
the sunny days and the cloudy days.
We believe that everything in life can be enjoyed.
You need just a little more awareness,
more consciousness of what is happening.
You are not your mind,
you are not your body.
There is a witness somewhere inside you
who can go on looking at the mind, at the emotions,
at the physiological reactions.
That witness is you.
And that witness is capable of enjoying everything,
once you get centered there.

—

Your mind feels misery, suffering; it feels all kinds of
emotions, attachments, desires and longings, but it is
all the projection of the mind.
Behind the mind is your real self, which has never
gone anywhere. It is always here and here.

—

Don't judge!

If you are angry, then be angry
– and don't judge that it is good or bad.
This is the difference between negative and positive
emotions: if you become aware of a certain emotion,
and by your becoming aware the emotion dissolves,
it is negative. If, by your becoming aware of a certain
emotion you then *become* the emotion, if the emotion
then spreads and becomes your being, it is positive.
Awareness works differently in each case.
If it is a poisonous emotion, you are relieved of it
through awareness. If it is good, blissful, ecstatic, you
become one with it. Awareness deepens it. So to me
this is the criterion: if something is deepened by your
awareness, it is something good.
If something is dissolved through awareness, it is
something bad.

That which cannot remain in awareness is sin, and
that which grows in awareness is virtue. Virtue and
sin are not social concepts, they are inner realiza-
tions.

~

I tell you that even negative emotions are good, if real; and if they are real, by and by, their very reality transforms them. They become more and more positive and a moment comes when all positivity and negativity disappears.

You simply remain authentic: you don't know what is good and what is bad, you don't know what is positive and what is negative. You are simply authentic. This authenticity will allow you to have a glimpse of the real.

Only the real can know the real, the true can know the truth, the authentic can know the authentic that surrounds you.

—

CHAPTER 2

emotions and sentimentality

Emotion is a purity; sentimentality is a trick.
You have learned a trick.

A woman knows that if she cries she is the winner.
Now, sometimes the crying is not coming at all
because crying is not so easily manipulated.
But she tries to bring it, she acts, she pretends.
Those tears are false.
Even if they are flowing through the eyes
they are false – because they are not coming,
they are being brought.
Sentimentality is emotion created,
manipulated,
cunningly.

Rationality is one thing;
rationalization is a manipulation of reason,
just as sentimentality is a manipulation of emotion.
If you are rational, *really* rational,
you will become a scientist.
If you are really emotional,
you will become a poet.
These are beautiful things.
But still, a real dialogue between a rational person and an emotional person will not be possible – it will be easier. With rationalization and sentimentality it is very difficult, but with reason and emotion it is not so difficult. Still there will be difficulties, but there will be compassion, an effort to understand each other.

~

Many people think that sentimentality is spirituality.

But emotions are as mental as thoughts, and what you call your heart is as much in your head as your head. You can become emotional very easily. You can cry and weep with tears falling down, big pearl-like tears – but it is nothing spiritual. Tears are as physical as anything else. The eyes are part of the body, and emotions are a disturbance in the physical energy.

You cry and weep – of course you will feel relieved, you will feel relaxed after you have had a good cry. You will feel relieved. All over the world, women know it. They know it well, that it helps. They cry and they weep and then they are relieved. It is a catharsis, but there is nothing spiritual in it. But people go on mistaking things – things which are not spiritual, they go on thinking they are spiritual.

~

Repression and Control

You never see animals going to war. Of course there are fights sometimes, but they are individual fights – not world wars with all the crows of the east fighting with all the crows of the west, or all the dogs of India fighting all the dogs of Pakistan. It is not. Dogs are not so foolish, neither are crows. Yes, sometimes they fight, and there is nothing wrong in it. If their freedom is violated they fight, but the fight is individual. It is not a world war.

Now, what have you done? You have repressed humanity and you have not allowed individuals to be angry sometimes – which is natural. The ultimate, total result is that everybody goes on gathering his anger, goes on repressing the anger, then one day everybody is so full of poison that it explodes in a world war. Every ten years a world war is needed.

And who is responsible for these wars?
Your so-called saints and moralists, do-gooders, the people who have never allowed you to be natural.

What is repression?

Repression is living a life that you were not meant to live, repression is doing things which you never wanted to do; repression is being the fellow that you are not. Repression is a way to destroy yourself, repression is suicide – very slow of course, but very certain, a slow poisoning.

Expression is life; repression is suicide.

———

Why? Why does man suppress so much and become unhealthy?

Through suppression, mind becomes split. The part that you accept becomes the conscious, and the part that you deny becomes the unconscious. This division is not natural, the division happens because of repression. And into the unconscious you go on throwing all the rubbish that society rejects – but remember, whatsoever you throw in there becomes more and more part of you. It goes into your hands, into your bones, into your blood, into your heartbeat.

Now psychologists say that almost eighty percent of diseases are caused by repressed emotions: so many heart failures means so much anger has been repressed in the heart, so much hatred that the heart is poisoned.

Why? Why does man suppress so much and become unhealthy? The society teaches you to control, not to transform, and the way of transformation is totally different. For one thing, it is not the way of control at all, it is just the opposite.

In controlling you repress, in transformation you express.

But there is no need to express it on somebody else because the "somebody else" is just irrelevant.

Next time you feel angry, go and run around the house seven times, and after it sit under a tree and watch where the anger has gone. You have not repressed it, you have not controlled it, you have not thrown it on somebody else – because if you throw it on somebody else a chain is created because the other is as foolish as you, as unconscious as you. If you throw it on another, and if the other is an enlightened person, there will be no trouble; he will help you to throw and release it and go through a catharsis. But if the other is as ignorant as you – if you throw anger on him he will react. He will throw more anger on you. He is repressed as much as you are. Then there comes a chain: you throw on him, he throws on you, and you both become enemies.

Don't throw it on anybody.

It is just like when you feel like vomiting: you don't go and vomit on somebody. Anger needs a vomit; you go to the bathroom and vomit – it cleanses the whole body. If you suppress the vomit it will be dangerous, and when you have vomited you will feel fresh, you will feel unburdened, unloaded, good, healthy. Something was wrong in the food that you have taken and the body rejects it.

Don't go on forcing it inside.

Anger is just a mental vomit. Something is wrong that you have taken in. Your whole psychic being wants to throw it out, but there is no need to throw it out on somebody. Because people throw it on somebody, society tells them to control it.

Reaction and Response

Whenever you are spontaneous it means you are not acting according to a preplanned idea.

In fact you were not ready, prepared, to do anything; the action has come as a response on its own accord.

You will have to understand these few words.

First is the distinction between reaction and response. Reaction is dominated by the other person. He insults you: you get angry, and then you act out of anger. This is reaction. You are not an independent person; anybody can pull you this way or that way. You are easily affected; you can be blackmailed emotionally. Reaction is an emotional blackmail. You were not angry. The man insulted you and his insult created anger; now out of anger comes your action. Response is out of freedom. It is not dependent on the other person. The other person may insult you, but you don't become angry. On the contrary, you meditate on the fact – why is he insulting you? Perhaps he is right. Then you have to be grateful to him, not get angry.

Perhaps he is wrong.
If he is wrong,
then for his wrong why should you burn your heart
with anger?

—

Emotions are not going to help you become
an integrated individuality.
They are not going to give you a granite soul.
You will remain just like a piece of deadwood
moving in the stream here and there,
not knowing why.

Emotions blind a person exactly as alcohol does.
They may have good names like *love*, they may have
bad names like *anger*, but once in a while you need
to be angry at someone, it relieves you.

In India you will sometimes see dogs making love on
the roads, and people hitting them with stones. Now
those poor fellows are not doing any harm to anybody
and they are performing a biological ritual that you
perform – they just don't have to hide in houses – and
they do so well. A crowd will move around them

throwing stones, beating them...strange behavior! People need to be angry once in a while, just as once in a while they need to be in love, and once in a while to hate someone.

~

A person who never becomes angry and goes on controlling his anger is very dangerous.
Beware of him, he can kill you. If your husband never becomes angry, report him to the police. A husband who sometimes becomes angry is just a nat-ural human being, there is no fear about it.

A husband who never becomes angry will one day suddenly jump and suffocate you.
And he will do it as if he is possessed by something.
Down through the ages murderers have been telling the courts,
"We committed the crime, but we were possessed."
Who possessed them? Their own unconscious, repressed unconscious, exploded.

~

Live, dance, eat, sleep...

Do things as totally as possible.
And remember again and again
that whenever you catch yourself
creating any problem,
slip out of it, immediately.

Once you get into the problem then a solution will
be needed. And even if you find a solution, out of
that solution a thousand and one problems will arise
again. Once you miss the first step you are in the
trap. Whenever you see that now you are slipping
into a problem catch hold of yourself, run, jump,
dance, but don't get into the problem. Do something
immediately so that the energy that was creating the
problems becomes fluid, unfrozen, melts, goes back
to the cosmos.

~

Sensitivity grows with awareness.

Through control you become dull and dead – that is part of the mechanism of control. If you are dull and dead then nothing will affect you, as if the body has become a citadel, a defence. Nothing will affect you, neither insult nor love. But this control is at a very great cost, an unnecessary cost, then it becomes the whole effort in life: how to control yourself – and then die! The whole effort of control takes all your energy, and then you simply die. The life becomes a dull and dead thing; you somehow carry on.

～

Mind can play the game of being silent.

It can play the game of being without any thoughts, any emotions, but they are just repressed, fully alive, ready to jump out any moment. The so-called religions and their saints have fallen into the fallacy of stilling the mind. If you go on sitting silently, trying to control your thoughts, not allowing your emotions, not allowing any movement within you, slowly it will become your habit.

This is the greatest deception in the world you can give to yourself, because everything is exactly the same, nothing has changed, but it appears as if you have gone through a transformation.

~

CHAPTER 3

anger

If you really want to know what anger is
go into it, meditate over it, taste it in many ways,
allow it to happen inside you,
be surrounded by it,
be clouded by it,
feel all the pang and the pain
and the hurt of it,
and the poison, and how it brings you low,
how it creates a dark valley for your being,
how you fall into hell through it,
how it is a downward flow.
Feel it, know it.
And that understanding will
start a transformation in you.

To know truth is to be transformed.

Truth liberates – but it must be your own.

———

What is anger?

The psychology of anger is that you wanted something, and somebody prevented you from getting it. Somebody came as a block, as an obstacle. Your whole energy was going to get something and somebody blocked the energy. You could not get what you wanted. Now this frustrated energy becomes anger – anger against the person who has destroyed the possibility of fulfilling your desire.

———

Your anger is true
because it belongs to you,
all that belongs to you is true.
So find the source of this anger,
where it is coming from.
Close your eyes and move inward;

before it is lost go backward to the source
-- and you will reach emptiness.

Go backward more, go inward more,
move deeper, and a moment comes
when there is no anger.
Inside, at the center, there is no anger.

From where does the anger come?

It never comes from your center, it comes from the
ego – and ego is a false entity.
If you go deeper you will find that your anger comes
from the periphery, not from the center. It cannot
come from the center, at the center is emptiness,
absolute emptiness. It comes only from the ego, and
ego is a false entity created by the society, it is a rela-
tivity, an identity. Suddenly you are whacked and the
ego feels hurt, anger is there.

~

People ARE angry.

Because they have suppressed so much anger, now there are no moments when they are not angry.

At the most, sometimes they are less angry, sometimes more.

Your whole being is poisoned by suppression. You eat with anger. When a person eats without anger it has a different quality, it is beautiful to watch him, because he eats nonviolently. He may be eating meat, but he eats nonviolently. You may be eating just vegetables and fruits, but if anger is suppressed you eat violently. Just through eating your teeth and your mouth release anger. You crush the food as if this is the enemy.

Next time you make love, watch: you will be doing the same movements as are done when you are aggressive. Watch the face, have a mirror around so you can see what is happening to your face – all the distortions of anger and aggression will be there.

In taking food, you become angry: look at a person eating. Look at a person making love – the anger has gone so deep that even love, an activity totally opposite to anger, even that is poisoned. Eating, an absolutely neutral activity, even that is poisoned. Then you just open the door and there is anger, you put a book on the table and there is anger, you take off the shoes and there is anger, you shake hands and there is anger – because now you are anger personified.

—

If you want to know anger
only to be rid of it, it is very difficult, because the attitude of being rid of anger creates a distinction. Then you have started with the assumption that anger is bad and "no-anger" is good; that sex is bad and "non-sexuality" is good; that greed is bad and "no-greed" is good. If you raise such distinctions, you will find a lot of difficulty to know the traits in actuality. Then even if you transcend them, it will only be repression.

—

A simple act of authentic spontaneity,
and immediately you are transported from this world
to another world. Love – or even anger... I tell you
that even positive emotions, false, are ugly; and even
negative emotions, authentic, are beautiful. Even
anger is beautiful when your whole being feels it,
when every fiber of your being is vibrant with it.

Look at a small child angry – and then you will feel the
beauty of it. His whole being is in it. Radiant, his face
red, such a small child looks so powerful that it seems
he could destroy the whole world! And what happens
to child once he is angry? After a few minutes, a few
seconds, everything is changed and he is happy and
dancing and running around the house again.

Why doesn't this happen to you?

You move from one falsity to another.

Really, anger is not a lasting phenomenon, by its very
nature it is a momentary thing.

If the anger is real it lasts for a few moments and,
while it lasts, authentic, it is beautiful. It harms
nobody.

A real, spontaneous thing cannot harm anybody. Only
falsity harms. In a man who can be angry spontaneously, the tide goes after a few seconds and he

relaxes perfectly to the very other extreme. He becomes infinitely loving.

~

Don't cut yourself in two.
I would suggest to be watchful, but if the time is not ripe you cannot be. Before you can be totally one with watchfulness you have to go through the hell of all your negative emotions, otherwise they will be repressed and they will erupt at any moment, at any weak time. So it is better to get rid of them. But getting rid of them does not mean that first you have to be watchful.

First, forget about watchfulness. Live each emotion that you feel; it is you. Hateful, ugly, unworthy – whatever it is, you be actually in it. First give them a chance to come up totally into the conscious.

Right now, by your effort of watchfulness you can repress them into the unconscious. And then you get involved in your day-to-day work and you force them back again. That is not the way to get rid of them. Let them come out – live them, suffer them.

It will be difficult and tedious but immensely rewarding. Once you have lived them, suffered them, accepted them, that this is you, that you have not made yourself in this way so you need not condemn yourself, that this is the way you have found yourself – once they are lived consciously, without any repression, you will be surprised that they are disappearing on their own. Their force on you is becoming less, their grip on your neck is no longer that tight. And when they are going away, there may be a time when you can start watching.

—

Remember not to misunderstand.

I have said, "Express your negative emotions," but I have not said, "publicly." That's how things become distorted.

Now if you are feeling angry with someone and you start expressing your anger, the other person is not going to be a Gautam Buddha and sit silently. He is not a marble statue, he will also do something. You will express anger, he will express anger. It will create more anger in you – and anger or violence create the same from the other side, and with a vengeance. Then you will feel like going into it more, because you have been told to express.

Yes, I have told you to express – but I don't mean publicly. If you are feeling angry go to your room, close off the room, beat the pillow, stand before a mirror, shout at your own image, say things that you have never said to anybody and always wanted to say. But it has to be a private phenomenon, otherwise there is no end.

Things go on moving in a circle, and we want to end them. So the moment you feel any negative emotion about anybody, that other person is not the question. The question is that you have a certain energy of anger. Now, that energy has to be diffused into the universe. You are not to repress it within yourself.

—

There is no need to throw it on anybody. You can go to your bathroom, you can go on a long walk – it means that something is inside that needs fast activity so that it is released. Just do a little jogging and you will feel it is released, or take a pillow and beat it, fight and bite the pillow until your hands and teeth are relaxed. Within a five-minute catharsis you will feel unburdened, and once you know this you will never throw it on anybody, because that is absolutely foolish.

Anger is beautiful; sex is beautiful.
But beautiful things can go ugly.
That depends on you.
If you condemn them, they become ugly;
if you transform them, they become divine.
Anger transformed becomes compassion
– because the energy is the same.
A buddha is compassionate:
from where does this compassion come?
This is the same energy that
was moving in anger;
now it is not moving in anger,
the same energy is transformed into compassion.

From where does love come?
A Buddha is loving; a Jesus is love.
The same energy that moves into sex becomes love.

So remember,
if you condemn a natural phenomenon
it becomes poisonous,
it destroys you, it becomes
destructive and suicidal.
If you transform it, it becomes divine.

But transformation is needed.

~

So-called "nonviolent" people
are the ugliest in the world.
They are not good people,
because they are holding down a volcano.
You cannot feel at ease with them.
Something is dangerously present there.
You can feel it, you can touch it;
it is oozing out of them.

~

If your anger is partial, lukewarm,

it is like a dog who is not certain how to behave with a stranger. He may be a friend of the master so he wags his tail; he may be an enemy, so he barks. He does both together. On one hand he goes on barking, on the other hand he goes on wagging his tail. He is playing the diplomat, so whatsoever the case turns out to be he can always feel right.

If the master comes and he sees that the master is friendly, the barking will stop and his whole energy will go into the tail. If the master is angry with the intruder, then the tail will stop completely and his whole energy will go into barking.

Your anger is also like that. You are weighing up how far to go, how much will pay; don't go beyond the limit, don't provoke the other person too much.

Pure anger has a beauty because it has totality. That's what happened to Jesus. When he went into the great temple and saw the moneychangers and their tables inside the temple he was in a rage. He became angry – the same anger that comes out of compassion and love. Single-handed, he drove all the moneychangers out of the temple and overturned their tables. He must have been really very angry, because driving all the moneychangers out of the temple single-handed is not an easy thing.

He must have been pure rage! Indians are upset about that. They cannot trust that Jesus is enlightened, just because of this incident.

People have their prejudices, their ideas. Rather than seeing into reality, rather than looking into an enlightened man, they come ready with so many concepts, and unless he fits them he is not enlightened. And let me tell you, no enlightened person is going to fit with your unenlightened prejudices; it is impossible.

—

Anger and sadness are the same

Sadness is passive anger and anger is active sadness. Because sadness comes easy, anger seems to be difficult. It is because you are too much in tune with the passive. It is difficult for a sad person to be angry. If you can make a sad person angry, his sadness will disappear immediately.
It will be very difficult for an angry person to be sad. If you can make him sad, his anger will disappear immediately.

In all our emotions the basic polarity continues – of man and woman, yin and yang, the male and the female. Anger is male, sadness is female. So if you are in tune with sadness, it is difficult to shift to anger, but I would like you to shift. Just exploding it within won't help much because again you are seeking some way of being passive. No. Bring it out, act it out. Even if it looks nonsense, then too. Be a buffoon in your own eyes, but bring it out.

If you can float between anger and sadness, both become similarly easy. You will have a transcendence, and then you will be able to watch. You can stand behind the screen and watch these games, and then you can go beyond both. But first you have to be moving easily between these two, otherwise you tend to be sad, and when one is heavy, transcendence is difficult.

Remember, when two energies, opposite energies,
are exactly alike, fifty-fifty,
then it is very easy to get out of them,
because they are fighting and canceling each other
and you are not in anybody's grip.
Your sadness and your anger are fifty-fifty, equal energies, so they cancel each other. Suddenly you have freedom and you can slip out. But if sadness is seventy percent and anger thirty percent then it is very difficult. Thirty percent anger in contrast with seventy percent sadness means forty percent sadness will still be there and it will not be possible, you will not be capable of easily slipping out. That forty percent will hang over you.

So this is one of the basic laws of inner energies – to always let the opposite polarities come to an equal status, and then you are able to slip out of them. It is as if two persons are fighting and you can escape.

They are so engaged with themselves that you need not worry, and you can escape.

⁓

Whatsoever is the case is the case.
Accept it and let it come – let it come in front of you.
In fact, just to say "do not repress" is not enough.
If you allow me, I would like to say, "Befriend it."
You are feeling sad? Befriend it.
Have compassion for it. Sadness also has a being.
Allow it, embrace it, sit with it, hold hands with it.
Be friendly. Be in love with it.
Sadness is beautiful! Nothing is wrong with it.
Who told you that something
is wrong in being sad?
In fact, only sadness gives you depth.
Laughter is shallow; happiness is skin-deep.
Sadness goes to the very bones,
to the marrow.
Nothing goes as deep as sadness.
So don't be worried. Remain with it and sadness will take you to your innermost core. You can ride on it and you will be able to know a few new things about your being that you had never known before. Those

things can be revealed only in a sad state, they can never be revealed in a happy state. Darkness is also good and darkness is also divine. The day is not only God's, the night is his also. I call this attitude religious.

—

To leave everything
and just sit under a tree and feel happy is not difficult – anybody will feel that way. Nothing to do, you can be detached; everything to do, you become attached. But when you do everything and remain unattached, when you move with the crowd, in the world and yet alone, then something real is happening.

If you don't feel anger when you are alone, that is not the point. When you are alone you will not feel anger because anger is a relationship, it needs some-body to be angry towards. Alone, unless you are mad you will not feel anger, it will be inside but it will not find any way to come out. When the other is there, then not to be angry is the point. When you don't have any money, any things, any house – if you are unattached, what is the difficulty in it? But when you have everything and you remain unattached –

a beggar in the palace – then something very deep has been attained.

If you move to the Himalayas and are unattached, you are a single note of the music;
if you live in the world and are attached, again you are a single note of the music.
But when you are in the world *and* beyond it, and you carry your Himalaya in the heart, you are a harmony, not a single note.

An accord happens, including all discordant notes, a synthesis of the opposites, a bridge between two banks.

And the highest is possible only when life is most complex; only in complexity the highest happens.

—

When you see anger in others,
go and dig within yourself
and you will find it there;
when you see too much ego in others, just go inside
and you will find ego sitting there.
The inside functions like a projector;
others become screens
and you start seeing films on others
which are really your own tapes.

~

The only problem with sadness,
desperation, anger, hopelessness, anxiety, anguish,
misery, is that you want to get rid of them. That's the
only barrier. You will have to live with them. You
cannot just escape. They are the very situation in
which life has to integrate and grow. They are the
challenges of life. Accept them. They are blessings in
disguise. If you want to escape from them, if you
somehow want to get rid of them, then a problem
arises – because if you want to get rid of something
you never look at it directly.

~

The star of a Broadway hit was visiting friends when talk got around, as usual, to psychiatry. "I must say," said the hostess, "I think my analyst is the best in the world. You can't imagine what he has done for me. You ought to try him."

"But I don't need analysis," said the star. "I could not be more normal – there is nothing wrong with me."

"But he is absolutely great," insisted her friend. "He will find something wrong."

There are people who live on finding something wrong with you. Their whole trade secret is to find something wrong with you. They cannot accept you as you are; they will give you ideals, ideas, ideologies, and they will make you feel guilty and they will make you feel worthless, dirt. In your own eyes, they will make you feel so condemned that you will forget all about freedom.

In fact you will become afraid of freedom, because you will see how bad you are, how wrong you are – and if you are free, you are going to do something wrong – so follow somebody. The priest depends on it, the politician depends on it. They give you right and wrong, fixed ideas, and then you will remain guilty forever.

~

There is nothing right
and nothing wrong

If you are angry, the priest will say anger is wrong,
don't be angry. What will you do? You can repress
anger, you can sit upon it, you can swallow it, literally, but it will go into you, into your system.
Swallow anger and you will have ulcers in the
stomach, swallow anger and sooner or later you will
have cancer. Swallow anger and you will have a
thousand and one problems arising out of it because
anger is poison. But what will you do? If anger is
wrong, you have to swallow it.

I don't say anger is wrong, I say anger is energy, pure
energy, beautiful energy. When anger arises, be aware
of it and see the miracle happen. When anger arises,
be aware of it and if you are aware you will be surprised, you are in for a surprise – maybe the greatest
surprise of your life – that as you become aware,
anger disappears. Anger is transformed. Anger
becomes pure energy; anger becomes compassion,
anger becomes forgiveness, anger becomes love. And
you need not repress, so you are not burdened by
some poison. And you are not being angry, so you

are not hurting anybody. Both are saved: the other, the object of your anger, is saved, and you are saved. In the past, either the object was to suffer, or you were to suffer.

What I am saying is that there is no need for anybody to suffer. Just be aware, let awareness be there. Anger will arise and will be consumed by awareness. One cannot be angry with awareness and one cannot be greedy with awareness and one cannot be jealous with awareness. Awareness is the golden key.

—

Try to understand why it is happening,
from where it is coming, where the roots are,
how it happens, how it functions,
how it overpowers you,
how in anger you become mad.
Anger has happened before,
it is happening now,
but now add a new element to it,
the element of understanding –
and then the quality will change.
Then, by and by, you will see
 that the more you understand anger,
the less it happens.
And when you understand it perfectly,
it disappears.
Understanding is like heat.
When the heat comes to a particular point
 – one hundred degrees –
the water disappears.

They say anger is bad.
Everyone has said to you that anger is bad, but no
one has told you how to know what anger is.

Everyone says sex is bad. They have been teaching,

teaching that sex is bad, and no one says what sex is and how to know it. Ask your father, and he will become uneasy. He will say, "Don't talk about such bad things." But these bad things are facts. Even your father could not escape it; otherwise you would not have been born. You are a naked fact. And no matter what your father says about sex, he couldn't escape it. But he will feel uneasy if you ask him because no one has told him; his parents never told him why sex is bad.

Why? And how to know it?
And how to go deep into it?
No one will tell this to you,
they will just go on labeling things:
this is bad and that is good.
That labeling creates misery and hell.

So one thing to remember –
for any seeker, a real seeker,
this is a basic thing to be understood:
remain with your facts,
try to know them.
Do not allow the society
to force its ideology on you.

Do not look at yourself
through others' eyes.
You have eyes; you are not blind.
And you have the facts
of your inner life.
Use your eyes!

~

Step within yourself without any prejudice,
without any assumptions, and see what is anger.
Let your anger reveal to you what anger is.
Do not impose your presumptions on it.
And the very day you discover anger
in its complete nakedness,
in its complete hideousness,
in its burning fire, in its murderous venom,
you will suddenly discover that you have stepped
out of it. Anger has vanished!
Any tendency can be treated this way –
which tendency, does not matter.
The process is the same because the illness is the
same, only the names are different.

~

Why do people get angry at you?

They are not angry at you, they are really afraid of you. And to hide the fear they have to project the anger. Anger is always to hide fear. People use all kinds of strategies. There are people who will laugh just so that they can stop their tears. In laughing you will forget, they will forget...and the tears can remain hidden. In anger, their fear remains hidden.

~

I am simply helping you to open up in all the dimensions, even if you feel that they are going against your ideas that you have held up to now. Even then, in fact more so, you will be available to them because this is a chance, an opportunity to judge whether whatsoever you have been thinking is right or not. It is a golden moment when you are encountered by something contrary to your ideas, thoughts, which up to now you have been thinking are rational. But if they are really rational then what is the fear?

It is fear that keeps people closed. They can't hear you – they are afraid to hear. And their anger is really their fear upside down. It is only a person who is full of fear who becomes immediately angry. If he does not become angry then you will be able to see his fear. Anger is a cover-up. By being angry he is trying to make you afraid: before you get any idea of his fear, he is trying to make you afraid. Do you see the simple psychology of it? He does not want you to know that he is afraid. The only way is to make you afraid; then he is completely at ease. You are afraid, he is not afraid – and there is nothing to be afraid of in a man who is afraid.

Their anger is an effort to deceive themselves. It has nothing to do with you.

—

But anger simply shows fear, remember always: anger is fear standing on its head. It is always fear that hides behind anger; fear is the other side of anger. Whenever you become afraid, the only way to hide the fear is to be angry because fear will expose you. Anger will create a curtain around you; you can hide behind.

—

CHAPTER 4

jealousy

Jealousy is comparison.
And we have been taught to compare,
we have been conditioned to compare,
always compare.
Somebody else has a better house,
somebody else has a more beautiful body,
somebody else has more money,
somebody else has a more charismatic personality.
Compare, go on comparing yourself
with everybody else you pass by,
and great jealousy will be the outcome;
it is the by-product of
the conditioning for comparison.

Otherwise, if you drop comparing, jealousy disappears. Then you simply know you are you, and you are nobody else, and there is no need. It is good that you don't compare yourself with trees, otherwise you will start feeling very jealous: why are you not green? And why has God been so hard on you – and no flowers? It is better that you don't compare with birds, with rivers, with mountains; otherwise you will suffer. You only compare with human beings, because you have been conditioned to compare only with human beings. You don't compare with peacocks and with parrots, otherwise, your jealousy would be more and more. You would be so burdened by jealousy that you would not be able to live at all.

Comparison is a very foolish attitude, because each person is unique and incomparable. Once this understanding settles in you, jealousy disappears. Each is unique and incomparable.

> You are just yourself.
> Nobody has ever been like you,
> and nobody will ever be like you.
> And you need not
> be like anybody else, either.

God creates only originals,
he does not believe in carbon copies.

～

Sex creates jealousy but it is a secondary thing.
So it is not a question of how to drop jealousy; you
cannot drop it because you cannot drop sex. The
question is how to transform sex into love, then jealousy disappears. If you love a person, the very love is
enough guarantee, the very love is enough security. If
you love a person, you know he cannot go to anybody else. And if he goes, he goes; nothing can be
done. What can you do? You can kill the person, but
a dead person will not be of much use.

When you love a person you trust that he cannot go
to anybody else. If he goes, there is no love and
nothing can be done. Love brings this understanding.
There is no jealousy. So if jealousy is there, know well
there is no love. You are playing a game, you are
hiding sex behind love. Love is just a painted word,
the reality is sex.

～

SOCIETY has exploited the individual in so many ways that it is almost impossible to believe. It has created devices so clever and cunning that it is almost impossible even to detect that they are devices. These devices are to exploit the individual, to destroy his integrity, to take away from him all that he has got – without even creating a suspicion in him, even a doubt about what is being done to him.

Jealousy is one of those tremendously powerful devices.

From the very childhood every society, every culture, every religion teaches everybody comparison.

Jealousy is one of the greatest devices. Look at it very closely: what does it mean?

Jealousy means to live in comparison. Somebody is higher than you, somebody is lower than you. You are always somewhere on a middle rung of the ladder. Perhaps the ladder is a circle because nobody finds the end of the ladder. Everybody is stuck somewhere in the middle, everybody is in the middle. The ladder seems to be a round wheel.

Somebody is above you – that hurts. That keeps you fighting, struggling, moving by any means possible, because if you succeed nobody cares whether you have succeeded rightly or wrongly. Success proves you are right; failure proves that you are wrong. All that matters is success, so any means will do. The end proves the means right. So you need not bother about means – and nobody does bother. The whole question is how to climb on up the ladder. But you never come to the end of it. And whosoever is above you is creating jealousy in you, that he has succeeded and you have failed.

A priori conclusions make you believers, not scientists.

When I say "meditate over it," I mean watch. Be a scientist in your inner world. Let your mind be your lab, and you observe – with no condemnation, remember. Don't say, "Jealousy is bad." Who knows? Don't say, "Anger is bad." Who knows? Yes, you have heard, you have been told, but that is what others say, this is not your experience. And you have to be very existential, experiential: unless your experiment proves it, you are not to say yes or no to anything. You have to be utterly non-judgmental. And then watching jealousy or anger or sex is a miracle.

What happens when you watch without any judgment? You start seeing through and through. Jealousy becomes transparent: you see the stupidity of it, you see the foolishness of it. Not that you have already decided that it is stupid; if you have decided you will miss the whole point. Remember it: I am not saying decide it is stupid, it is foolish. If you decide, you miss the whole point. You simply go without any decision, just to see exactly what it is.

What is this jealousy?

What is this energy called jealousy? And watch it as you watch a roseflower – just look into it. When there is no conclusion your eyes are clear; the clarity is attained only by those who have no conclusions. Watch, look into it, and it will become transparent, and you *will* come to know that it is stupid. And knowing its stupidity, it drops of its own accord. You don't need to drop it.

~

You cannot even see the other person being happy with someone for a minute – and you think you can die for the other person? Just try to see what actually is in you for the other person – and jealousy will disappear. In most of the cases with jealousy your love will also disappear. But it is good, because what is the point of having a love which is full of jealousy, which is not love?

If jealousy disappears and love still remains, then you have something solid in your life which is worth having.

~

Jealousy is one of the most prevalent areas of psychological ignorance about yourself, about others and more particularly, about relationship. People think they know what love is – they do not know. And their misunderstanding about love creates jealousy. By "love" people mean a certain kind of monopoly, some possessiveness – without understanding a simple fact of life: that the moment you possess a living being you have killed that person.

Life cannot be possessed.
You cannot have it in your fist.
If you want to have it,
you have to keep your hands open.

What makes you jealous?

Jealousy itself is not the root.

You love a woman, you love a man; you want to possess the man or the woman just out of fear that perhaps tomorrow he may move with somebody else. The fear of tomorrow destroys your today, and it is a vicious circle. If every day is destroyed because of the fear of tomorrow, sooner or later the man is going to look for some other woman because you are just a pain in the neck. And when he starts looking for another woman or starts moving with another woman, you think your jealousy has proved right. In fact it is your jealousy that has created the whole thing.

So the first thing to remember is: Don't be bothered about tomorrows; today is enough.

Somebody loves you...let this be a day of joy, a day of celebration. Be so totally in love today that your totality and your love will be enough for the man not to move away from you. Your jealousy will move him away; only your love can keep him with you. His jealousy will move you away; his love can keep you with him.

Don't think of tomorrow. The moment you think of tomorrow your living today remains half-hearted. Just live today and leave tomorrow, it will take its own course. And remember one thing, that if today has been such a beauty of experience, such a blessing – out of today is born tomorrow, so why be worried about it?

If some day the man you have loved, the woman you have loved finds somebody else – it is simply human to be happy, but your woman is happy with somebody else – it does not make any difference whether she is happy with you or happy with somebody else, she is happy. And if you love her so much how can you destroy her happiness?

A real love will always be happy if the partner feels joyous with somebody else. In this situation – when a woman is with somebody else, and you are still happy and you are still grateful to the woman and you still tell the woman, "You have absolute freedom; just be totally happy, that is my happiness. With whom you are happy is insignificant, what is significant is your happiness" – my feeling is that she cannot remain away from you for long, she will be back. Who can leave such a man or such a woman?

Your jealousy destroys everything. Your possessive-ness destroys everything.

~

This is a universal problem
and it cannot be solved, it can only be transcended. People try to solve it. They create more problems; that's what is being done all over the world. These problems – jealousy, possessiveness – are not really problems but symptoms, symptoms that you don't yet know what love is. We take it for granted that we know what love is, and then the problem of jealousy arises. That is not right. The problem is arising because love is not yet there. It simply shows that love has not yet arrived, it simply shows the absence of love. So you cannot solve it.

All that is needed is to forget about jealousy, because that is a negative fight. It is fighting with darkness; it is pointless. Rather, light a candle. That's what love is. Once love starts flowing, jealousy and possessive-ness and all that simply become nonexistent. You are simply surprised at where they have gone, you cannot find them. It is just as when you light a candle you can go on looking for darkness all over the room and you will not find it. You are even looking with a light and you cannot find it. You cannot find it with light because it is no longer there; it was simply an absence of light. Jealousy is absence of love.

My approach is: don't be bothered about jealousy, otherwise you will be getting into such a trap that you will never be able to get out of. Forget about it! It is symptomatic, it is simply indicative. It is good that it indicates something; it is a signal that love has not yet happened. It is good. Learn something from it, take note of it and start moving into love. Enjoy love more and there will be less jealousy. Delight in love more and there will be still less jealousy. Let your love become a totality, a madness. Let it have an intensity, and in that intensity jealousy will be burned out.

A real lover has never known what jealousy is. So I will not say to start doing something about jealousy; no, not at all. Thank it because it simply shows something that has to happen has not happened. Put more energy into love. Rather than putting energy into analyzing jealousy and fighting with it, put more energy into love. Otherwise you will be distracted: you will start following jealousy, and that is a desert, you will never come to its end. That's where the whole of psychoanalysis has got stuck: it takes symptoms as problems and then starts penetrating those symptoms, analyzing. You can go on peeling the onion, you can go on and on, one layer after another layer, and after that another layer.

Have you come across a person who is really psychoanalyzed? Not a single person exists on the earth whose psychoanalysis is complete. It cannot be. Year in and year out you can go to the psychoanalyst, and there is always something that you have to explore. It is a futile direction, it takes you sideways. Go straight into love.

Make love a great celebration.
Put your total energy into it
with no thought of the future.
While you are in love with anybody,
don't hold back.
If you hold back in the moment, that will become jealousy. If you go totally into it when you are

making love, without holding anything, if you are utterly lost in it, your whole body and being becomes orgasmic; you are wild, screaming and singing and crying and weeping and laughing all together, you will feel such peace arising out of it that nothing can distract you, nothing can disturb you. Make love a feast and these things like jealousy will disappear.

Jealousy has nothing to do with love

In fact your so-called love also has nothing to do with love. These are beautiful words which you use without knowing what they mean, without experiencing what they mean. You go on using the word *love*. You use it so much that you forget the fact that you have not experienced it yet. That is one of the dangers of using such beautiful words: *God*, *love*, *nirvana*, *prayer* – beautiful words. You go on using them, you go on repeating them, and by and by the very repetition makes you feel as if you know.

What do you know about love?

Jealousy is never present in love.
And wherever jealousy is present,
love is not present.
Jealousy is not part of love,
jealousy is part of possessiveness.
Possessiveness has nothing to do with love.
You want to possess.
Through possession you feel strong: your territory is bigger.
And if somebody else tries to trespass on your territory, you are angry.

Or if somebody has a bigger house than your house, you are jealous.
Or if somebody tries to dispossess you of your property, you are jealous and angry.
If you love, jealousy is impossible; it is not possible at all.

—

Jealousy is like a rock – very gross.
Possessiveness is a rock – it is pure poison. Love is destroyed, crushed, shattered. And these monsters are dominating people. Love has to be freed from these monsters. The only way is to kill the root cause.

—

If you can destroy jealousy, kill it, you will see such beautiful energies arising in you.

Love
becomes so easy if you can destroy jealousy;
otherwise jealousy destroys love.

If you destroy hate, suddenly you have so much love

that you become unconditional. You don't bother about whether the person is worthy of love or not. Who bothers when you have too much to give? You simply give and you feel grateful that he accepted.

~

And the moment
Adam and Eve had eaten
from the tree of knowledge
God drove them out of heaven,
out of paradise,
because of the fear that now
they would try the other tree.
And once they ate
from the other tree they
would become immortal,
they would be like gods.
That means that
God felt jealous.
They have become half
like God because now
they know they are not
immortal. Then there
would be no difference

between God and them:
they would know;
God knows.
They would be immortal;
God is immortal.
So a great jealousy
arose in God's mind.
It was out of jealousy that Adam and Eve
were thrown out of paradise.
This is not a very healthy
concept of God.

—

Your gods cannot be different from you. Who will create them? Who will give them shape and color and form? You create them, you sculpt them; they have eyes like you, noses like you – and minds like you!

The Old Testament God says: "I am a very jealous God."

Now who has created this God who is jealous? God cannot be jealous. And if God is jealous, then what is wrong in being jealous? If even God is jealous, why should you be thought to be doing something wrong when you are jealous? Then jealousy is divine!

~

Jealousy means somebody else has more than you have. And it is impossible to be the first in everything. You may have the largest amount of money in the world, but you may not have a beautiful face. And a beggar may make you jealous – his body, his face, his eyes, and you are jealous. A beggar can make an emperor jealous.

~

Your whole life you have been jealous. What have you learned out of it?

If you are not learning out of these experiences, you will have to repeat your life again.

Learn out of every experience, small or big. Whenever you are jealous you are in a fire, your heart burns – and you know what you are doing to yourself. You know the wrongness of it, but you know it only because others say so. It is not your own under-standing, your own insight. Let it become your own insight so the next time the situation arises to be jealous you can laugh at it, so the next time the same situation arises you don't behave in the same old pattern; you can get out of the old pattern.

~

Your jealousy will destroy your energy unnecessarily. Rather than being jealous, find out what you can do with your energy, what you can create.

~

CHAPTER 5

fear

What is this fear?

There is only one basic fear.

All other small fears are byproducts of the one main fear that every human being carries with himself.

The fear of losing yourself.

It may be in death, it may be in love, but the fear is the same: You are afraid of losing yourself. And the strangest thing is that only those people are afraid of losing themselves who don't have themselves.

Those who have themselves are not afraid.

So it is really a question of exposure.

You don't have anything to lose; you just believe that you have something to lose.

—

People are afraid of life, and they are afraid of life because life is only possible if you are capable of being wild.

wild in your love,

wild in your song,

wild in your dance.

This is where fear is.

Who is afraid of death? I have never come across such a person. And almost every person I have come across is afraid of life.

Drop fear of life. Because either you can be afraid or you can live; it is up to you. And what is there to be afraid of? You can't lose anything. You have everything to gain. Drop all fears and jump totally into life. Then, one day, death will come as a welcome guest, not your enemy, and you will enjoy death more than you have enjoyed life because death has its own beauties. And death is very rare because it happens once in a while – life is every day.

It's a good kind of fear if you don't know what exactly it is.

That simply means that you are on the verge of something unknown. When the fear has some object it is an ordinary fear. One is afraid of death – it is very ordinary fear, instinctive; nothing great about it, nothing special about it. When one is afraid of old age or disease, illness, these are ordinary fears, common, garden variety.

The special fear is when you cannot find an object to it, when it is there for no reason at all; that makes one *really* scared!

If you can find a reason, the mind is satisfied. If you can answer why, the mind has some explanation to cling to. All explanations help things to be explained away; they don't do anything else. But once you have a rational explanation you feel satisfied. That's why people go to the psychoanalyst to find explanations. Even a stupid explanation is better than nothing; one can cling to the explanation.

You have fear – don't ask why.

—

Fear is natural, guilt is a creation of the priests.
Guilt is man-made.
Fear is in-built, and it is very essential.
Without fear you will not be able to survive at all.
Fear is normal.

It is because of fear that you will not put your hand in
the fire. It is because of fear that you will walk to the
right or to the left, whatsoever is the law of the country.
It is because of fear that you will avoid poison. It is
because of fear that when the truck driver sounds his
horn, you run out of the way.

If the child has no fear there is no possibility that he
will ever survive. His fear is a life-protective measure.
But because of this natural tendency to protect
oneself...and nothing is wrong in it – you have the
right to protect yourself. You have such a precious life
to protect and fear simply helps you.

Fear is intelligence.
Only idiots don't have fear, imbeciles don't have
fear; hence you have to protect the idiots, otherwise
they will burn themselves or they will jump out of
a building, or they will go into the sea without

knowing how to swim or they can eat a snake...or they can do anything.

Fear can become abnormal, it can become pathological. Then you are afraid of things of which there is no need to be afraid – although you can find arguments even for your abnormal fear. For example, somebody is afraid of going inside a house. Logically you cannot prove that he is wrong. He says, "What is the guarantee that the house will not fall?" Another person is afraid – he cannot travel because there are train accidents. Somebody else is afraid and cannot go into a car because there are car accidents. And somebody else is afraid of an airplane. If you become afraid in this way, this is not intelligent. Then you should be afraid of your bed too, because almost ninety-seven percent of people die in their beds! That is the most dangerous place to be in, logically you should remain as far away from the bed as possible, never go close to it. But then you will make your life impossible.

~

Everything has energy:
Fear
anger
jealousy
hate.
You are unaware
of the fact
that all these things
are wasting
your life.

~

The fear of death
is not the fear of death,
it is a fear of remaining unfulfilled.
You are going to die, and nothing, nothing at all
could you experience through life – no maturity, no
growth, no flowering.
Empty-handed you came,
empty-handed you are going.
This is the fear.

~

When you are grown up you can see – you can try to
peel the onion layer by layer – how fears have been
created in you, how gullible you have been, how
people have exploited your innocence. The priest
had no knowledge of God, yet he deceived you
and pretended that he knows God. He had no idea
of heaven and hell, yet he forced you to be afraid of
hell, to be ambitious for heaven. He created greed, he
created fear. He himself was a victim of other people.
Now you can look back: your father was not aware
what he was teaching, what he was telling to you...

~

There are fears, and there is that constant urge to seek and to search. And I hope that the fears will not be the winners, because anybody who lives out of fears, lives not; he is already dead. Fear is part of death, not of life.

Risk, adventure, going into the unknown, is what life means. So try to understand your fears. And remember one thing: don't support them, they are your enemies. Support the urge that is still alive in you, make it aflame so that it can burn all those fears and you can move into seeking.

~

Nobody wants to be lonely

Everybody wants to belong to a crowd –
not only one crowd, but many crowds.

A person belongs to a religious crowd, a political party, a Rotary Club... and there are many other small groups to belong to. One wants to be supported twenty-four hours a day because the false, without support, cannot stand. The moment one is alone, one starts feeling a strange craziness.

It is not only your fear, it is everybody's fear. Because nobody is what he was supposed to be by existence. The society, the culture, the religion, the education have all been conspiring against innocent children. They have all the powers – the child is helpless and dependent. So whatsoever they want to make out of him, they manage to do it. They don't allow any child to grow to his natural destiny. Their every effort is to make human beings into utilities.

If a child is left on his own to grow, who knows whether he will be of any use to the vested interests or not? The society is not prepared to take the risk. It grabs the child and starts molding him into some-thing that is needed by the society. In a certain sense, it kills the soul of the child and gives him a false identity so that he never misses his soul, his being. The false identity is a substitute.

But that substitute is useful only in the same crowd which has given it to you. The moment you are alone, the false starts falling apart and the repressed real starts expressing itself. Hence the fear of being lonely.

You believed yourself to be somebody, and then suddenly in a moment of loneliness you start feeling you are not that. It creates fear: then who are you? It will take some time for the real to express itself. The gap between the two has been called by the mystics "the dark night of the soul."

A very appropriate expression. You are no more the false, and you are not yet the real. You are in a limbo, you don't know who you are. Particularly in the West the problem is even more complicated, because they have not developed any methodology to discover the real as soon as possible so that the dark night of the soul can be shortened. The West knows nothing as far as meditation is concerned.

And meditation is only a name

for being alone, silent,

waiting for the real to assert itself.

It is not an act,

it is a silent relaxation –

because whatever you *do*

will come out of your false personality.

Years of a false personality imposed by people who you loved, who you respected...and they were not intentionally doing anything bad to you. Their intentions were good, just their awareness was nil. They were not conscious people – your parents, your teachers, your priests, your politicians – they were not conscious people, they were unconscious. And even a good intention in the hands of an unconscious person turns out to be poisonous.

So whenever you are alone, a deep fear – because suddenly the false starts disappearing.

And the real will take a little time. You have lost it years back. You will have to give some consideration to the fact that this gap has to be bridged.

—

The crowd is an essential for the false self to exist.

The moment it is lonely, you start freaking out. This is where one should understand a little bit of meditation. Don't be worried, because that which can disappear is worth disappearing. It is meaningless to cling to it – it is not yours, it is not you.

Nobody else can answer your question "Who am I?"
You will know it.
All meditative techniques are a help
to destroy the false.
They don't give you the real –
the real cannot be given.
That which can be given cannot be real.
The real you have got already;
just the false has to be taken away.

Meditation is just a courage
to be silent and alone.
Slowly slowly, you start feeling a
new quality to yourself,
a new aliveness,
a new beauty,

a new intelligence
which is not borrowed from anybody,
which is growing within you.
It has roots in your existence.
And if you are not a coward
it will come to fruition,
to flowering.

~

All your fears are by-products of identification

You love a woman and with the love, in the same parcel, comes fear: she may leave you – she has already left somebody and come with you. There is a precedent; perhaps she will do the same to you. There is fear, you feel knots in the stomach. You are too much attached. You cannot get a simple fact:

You have come alone in the world; you have been here yesterday also, without this woman, perfectly well, without any knots in the stomach. And tomorrow if this woman goes...what is the need of the knots? You know how to be without her, and you will be able to be without her.

The fear that things may change tomorrow...

Somebody may die, you may go bankrupt, your job may be taken away. There are a thousand and one things which may change. You are burdened with fears and fears, and none of them are valid – because yesterday also you were full of all these fears, unnecessarily. Things may have changed, but you are still alive. And man has an immense capacity to adjust himself in any situation.

Fear is like darkness.

What can you do about darkness directly? You cannot drop it, you cannot throw it out, you cannot bring it in. There is no way to relate with darkness without bringing light in.

The way to darkness goes via light. If you want darkness, put the light off; if you don't want darkness, put the light on. But you will have to do something with light, not with darkness at all.

All men are afraid of women,
and all women are afraid of men – because all people
are afraid of love. The fear is of love.
Hence man is afraid of woman because she is the
object of love, and women are afraid of men because
they are the object of their love.

We are afraid of love because love is a small death.
Love requires that we should surrender, and we
don't want to surrender at all. We would like the
other to surrender, we would like the other to be a
slave. But the same is the desire from the other side:
man wants the woman to be a slave; and of course
the woman also wants the same, the same desire is
there. Their methods of enslaving each other may be
different, but the desire is the same.

~

All fears can be reduced to one fear:

the fear of death, the fear that, "One day I may have to disappear, one day I may have to die. I am, and the day is coming when I will not be" – that frightens, that is the fear. To avoid that fear we start moving in such a way so that we can live as long as possible. And we try to secure our lives – we start compromising, we start becoming more and more secure, safe, because of the fear. We become paralyzed, because the more secure you are, the more safe you are, the less alive you will be.

So because of the fear of death we strive for security, for a bank balance, for insurance, for marriage, for a settled life, for a home; we become part of a country, we join a political party, we join a religious church – we become Hindus, Christians, Mohammedans. These are all ways to find security. These are all ways to find some place to belong to – a country, a church.

Because of this fear politicians and priests go on exploiting you. If you are not in any fear no politician, no priest can exploit you. It is only out of fear that he can exploit because he can provide – at least he can promise – that this will make you secure:

"This will be your security. I can guarantee."
The goods may never be delivered – that's another thing – but the promise... And the promise keeps people exploited, oppressed.
The promise keeps people in bondage.

—

Fear is made of ignorance of one's own self.
There is only one fear;
it manifests in many ways,
a thousand and one
can be the manifestations,
but basically fear is one,
and that is that
"Deep inside, I may not be."
And in a way it is true
that you are not.

—

Courage means going into the unknown
in spite of all the fears.
Courage does not mean fearlessness.
Fearlessness happens if you go on being courageous
and more courageous. That is the ultimate experience
of courage – fearlessness; that is the fragrance when
the courage has become absolute.
But in the beginning there is not much difference
between the coward and the courageous person.
The only difference is, the coward listens to his fears
and follows them, and the courageous person puts
them aside and goes ahead.
The courageous person goes into the unknown in spite
of all the fears. He knows the fears, the fears are there.

～

You have exaggerated your fears.
Just look at them, and just by your looking at them
they will start becoming smaller.

You have never looked at them.
You have been escaping from them. You have been
creating protections against them, rather than looking
directly into the eyes of your fear.

There is nothing to fear at all; all that is needed is a little more awareness. So whatever your fear is, catch hold of it, look at it minutely, the way a scientist looks at a thing. And you will be surprised, it starts melting like an ice flake. By the time you have looked into its totality, it is gone. And when freedom is there without any fear, it brings such benediction that there are no words to express it.

—

Fear accepted becomes freedom

Fear denied, rejected, condemned, becomes guilt. If you accept fear as part of the situation...

It *is* part of the situation. Man is a part, a very small, tiny part, and the whole is vast. Man is a drop, a very small drop, and the whole is the whole ocean. A trembling arises: "I may be lost in the whole; my identity may be lost."

That is the fear of death. All fear is the fear of death. And the fear of death is the fear of annihilation.

~

A man living out of fear is always trembling inside. He is continuously on the point of going insane, because life is big, and if you are continuously in fear... And there is every kind of fear. You can make a big list and you will be surprised how many fears are there – and still you are alive! There are infections all around, diseases, dangers, kidnapping, terrorists... and such a small life. And finally there is death, which you cannot avoid.

Your whole life will become dark. Drop the fear! The fear was taken up by you in your childhood unconsciously; now consciously drop it and be mature. And then life can be a light which goes on deepening as you go on growing.

—

CHAPTER 6

**understanding is
the secret of transformation**

Just be a little more understanding
of all your sentiments, emotions.
They all have a certain place
in the total harmony of your being.
But we have been kept almost blind
to our own potentialities, dimensions.

Be a little more alert about everything,
and remember
that the natural is the superior,
and the unnatural
is phony and American.

～

From the very beginning one should remember that we are in search of a place, a space, where nothing arises – no dust, no smoke; where everything is pure and clean, utterly empty, just spaciousness. One should be clear from the very beginning what we are looking for.

—

Awareness is needed, not condemnation

Through awareness transformation happens spontaneously. If you become aware of your anger, understanding penetrates. Just watching, with no judgment, not saying good, not saying bad, just watching in your inner sky.

There is lightning, anger,
you feel hot,
the whole nervous system shaking and quaking,
and you feel a tremor all over the body –
a beautiful moment, because when energy functions
you can watch it easily; when it is not functioning you cannot watch.

Close your eyes and meditate on it. Don't fight, just look at what is happening – the whole sky filled with electricity, so much lightning, so much beauty – just lie down on the ground and look at the sky and watch.

Then do the same inside. Clouds are there, because without clouds there can be no lightning.
Dark clouds are there, thoughts. Somebody has insulted you, somebody has laughed at you, some-body has said this or that...many clouds, dark clouds in the inner sky and much lightning.

Watch! It is a beautiful scene – terrible also, because you don't understand. It is mysterious, and if mystery is not understood it becomes terrible, you are afraid of it. And whenever a mystery is understood it becomes a grace, a gift, because now you have the keys – and with keys you are the master.

You don't control it, you simply become a master when you are aware. And the more you become aware the more inward you penetrate, because awareness is a going-inward, it always goes inward: more aware, more in; totally aware, perfectly in; less aware, more out; unconscious – you are completely out, out of your house wandering around.

—

The Empty Heart

People have always thought that "mind" means word, speech, thoughts – but that is not true. They are very close, concurrent, so close that you can get the conception that they are one. But when you get deeper into meditation and leave the world of words and speech, you suddenly find there is an empty mind beyond them which is your real mind. To distinguish it, we call it the empty heart.

Either to call it no-mind, real-mind, empty heart... they are all synonymous. But ordinarily you are so close to thinking, emotions, words, that you cannot conceive there is a sky beyond the clouds, that there is a full moon beyond the clouds. You will have to go beyond the clouds to see the moon.

—

The empty heart
is a door to eternity.
It is a connection between you
and existence.
It is not something physical
or material.
It is not something mental
or psychological.
It is something beyond both,
transcending both.
It is your spirituality.
Remember, the empty heart
makes you a buddha.

Understanding is the secret of transformation. If you can understand anger, immediately you will be showered with compassion. If you can understand sex, immediately you will attain to superconsciousness. *Understanding* is the most important word to remember.

—

You feel anger, you feel jealousy, you feel hatred, you feel lust. Is there any technique that can help you to get rid of anger? of jealousy? of hatred? of sexual lust? And if these things continue to remain, your lifestyle is going to remain the same as before.

There is only one way – there has never been a second. There is one and only one way to understand that to be angry is to be stupid: watch anger in all its phases, be alert to it so it does not catch you unawares; remain watchful, seeing every step of the anger. And you will be surprised: that as awareness about the ways of anger grows, the anger starts evaporating.

And when the anger disappears, then there is a peace. Peace is not a positive achievement.

When the hatred disappears, there is love. Love is not a positive achievement.

When jealousy disappears, there is a deep friendliness toward all.

Try to understand... But all the religions have corrupted your minds because they have not taught you how to watch, how to understand; instead they have given you conclusions – that anger is bad. And the moment you condemn something, you have already taken a certain position of judgment.

You have judged. Now you cannot be aware.

Awareness needs a state of no-judgment. And all the religions have been teaching people judgments: this is good, this is bad, this is sin, this is virtue – this is the whole crap that for centuries man's mind has been loaded with. So, with everything – the moment you see it – there is immediately a judgment about it within you. You cannot simply see it, you cannot be just a mirror without saying anything.

Understanding arises by becoming a mirror, a mirror of all that goes on in the mind.

Why do you think about renouncing anger? Why? Because you have been taught that anger is bad. But have *you* understood it as bad? Have *you* come to a personal conclusion, through your own deepening insight, that anger is bad?

If you have come to this conclusion through your own inner search, there will be no need to quit it – it will have already disappeared. The very fact of knowing that this is poisonous is enough. Then you are a different person.

⁓

You go on thinking of leaving, quitting, renouncing. Why? Because people say that anger is bad, and you are simply influenced by whatsoever they say. Then you go on thinking that anger is bad, and when the moment comes you go on being angry.

This is how a double mind is created: you remain with anger, and yet you always think anger is bad. This is inauthenticity. If you think that anger is good, then do it and do not say that anger is bad. Or if you say anger is bad, then try to understand whether this is your realization or whether someone else has said it to you.

Everyone is creating misery around himself because of others. Someone says this is bad and someone says that it is good, and they go on forcing these ideas in your mind. The parents are doing this, the society is doing this, and then one day you are just following others' ideas.

And the difference between your nature and others' ideas cause a split; you become schizophrenic. You will do something and you will believe in the very contrary. That will create guilt. Everyone feels guilty. Not that everyone *is* guilty, everyone feels guilty because of this mechanism.

~

Whenever there is joy,
you feel that it is coming from without. You have met a friend: of course, it appears that the joy is coming from your friend, from seeing him. That is not the actual case.

The joy is always within you.
The friend has just become a situation. The friend has helped it to come out, has helped you to see that it is there. And this is not only with joy, but with

everything: with anger, with sadness, with misery, with happiness, with everything, it is so. Others are only situations in which things that are hidden in you are expressed. They are not causes; they are not causing something in you. Whatsoever is happening, is happening *to you*. It has always been there; it is only that meeting with this friend has become a situation in which whatsoever was hidden has come out in the open – has come out. From the hidden sources it has become apparent, manifest. Whenever this happens remain centered in the inner feeling, and then you will have a different attitude about everything in life.

Whenever you are alone,

there is nobody to provoke your anger, nobody to create an opportunity where you can become sad, nobody to bring your own false faces before you. You are alone: anger does not arise. Not that anger has disappeared – simply the situation for anger is not there. You are full of anger, but nobody is there to insult you, to hurt you. Only the opportunity is missing. Come back to the world: live fifty years in the Himalayas – when you come back to the world, immediately you will find anger is there, as fresh as ever; even maybe more powerful now because of fifty years accumulated anger, accumulated poison. Then one becomes afraid to come back to the world.

Go to the Himalayas: you will see many people hanging around there. Cowards, they cannot come back to the world. What sort of purity is this, which is afraid? What sort of celibacy is this, which is afraid? What sort of reality is this, which is afraid of *maya*, of illusion? What sort of light is this, which is afraid of darkness: that it comes to the dark, the darkness will be powerful and may destroy it? Has darkness ever destroyed any light? But they go on hanging around. The more they hang around there, the more they become incapable of coming back to the world – because there in the Himalayas they can have their beautiful image: nobody else to destroy it. In the world it is difficult. Somebody, from somewhere, treads on your toe; somebody, from somewhere, hurts you. You have to drop anger. My whole effort is so that you change.

Don't try to change the scene, please change yourself.

The change of the scene not going to help anybody; it has never helped anybody. Even if you meditate twenty-four hours a day it is not going to help unless meditation becomes a way of life – not that you meditate. Whether you meditate one hour, or two hours, or three hours, or six hours, or many hours – you may meditate twenty-four hours: you will go mad, but you will not attain to *samadhi*.

—

CHAPTER 7

methods to help you

[The following chapter includes practical suggestions for individual experiments in the world of emotions.]

What's Your Issue?

My method is so simple.

Just put down in your diary for seven days, noting every day what it is that takes most of your time, what it is that becomes your fantasy most of the time, where your energy always moves readily. And just watching for seven days, noting in your notebook, you can find your own chief characteristic. And this finding is half the victory. It gives you a great strength, that you know the enemy.

—

The lotus is one of the most miraculous phenomena in existence; hence in the East it has become the symbol of spiritual transformation. Buddha is seated on a lotus, Vishnu is standing on a lotus.

Why a lotus? – because the lotus has one very symbolic significance: it grows out of the mud.

It is a transformation symbol, it is a metamorphosis. The mud is dirty, maybe stinking; the lotus is fragrant, and it has come out of the stinking mud.

Exactly in the same way [says Buddha], life ordinarily is just stinking mud – but the possibility of becoming a lotus is hidden there.

The mud can be transformed, you can become a lotus.

Sex can be transformed and it can become *samadhi*.

Anger can be transformed and it can become compassion.

Hate can be transformed and it can become love.

Everything that you have that looks negative right now, mudlike, can be transformed.

Your noisy mind can be emptied and transformed, and it becomes celestial music.

~

Transformation of Anger

PILLOW MEDITATION

When: Every Morning
Duration: 20 minutes

The first thing in transforming anger is to express it, but not on anybody, because if you express it on somebody you cannot express it totally.
You may like to kill, but it is not possible;
you may like to bite, but it is not possible.
But that can be done to a pillow.

The pillow will not react, and the pillow will not go to any court,
and the pillow will not bring any enmity against you,
and the pillow will not *do* anything.
The pillow will be happy, and the pillow will laugh at you.

The second thing to remember: be aware.
In controlling, no awareness is needed; you simply do it mechanically, like a robot. The anger comes and there is a mechanism – suddenly your whole being

becomes narrow and closed. If you are watchful, control may not be so easy. Society never teaches you to be watchful, because when somebody is watchful he is wide open. That is part of awareness – one is open, and if you want to suppress something and you are open, it is contradictory, it may come out. The society teaches you how to close yourself in, how to cave yourself in – don't allow even a small window for anything to go out.

But remember: when nothing goes out, nothing comes in either. When the anger cannot go out, you are closed. If you touch a beautiful rock nothing goes in; you look at a flower, nothing goes in, your eyes are dead and closed. You kiss a person, nothing goes in because you are closed. You live an insensitive life. Sensitivity grows with awareness.

~

SEARCH FOR THE ROOTS

You are feeling sad or angry,
you can make it a meditation.
Don't fight it, don't try to distract your mind into

something else. Don't go to see a movie because you are feeling very sad. Don't try to repress your feeling. It is a great opportunity for meditation.

Just watch from where the anger arises. Just go to the very roots. Just go to the very roots from where the sadness is coming – and the greatest surprise is that they don't have any roots.

So when you look for their roots, by that time they start disappearing seeing that, "This man is strange – he is looking for the roots!" And those afflictions, emotions, sentiments, feelings – none of them have any roots. They are just clouds, without any roots, surrounding your mind.

And if you start looking for roots the emotions start dispersing – "This is not the right person, he is not going to be affected by us. He is a little strange; here we are, and he is looking for the roots!" Rather than being sad, rather than being angry, rather than being miserable, he is searching for the roots.

Every sentiment, every emotion, every feeling will disappear if you look for the roots. If your awareness goes that deep in search then that emotion will be gone, and the sky of your inner being will be absolutely clear and clean. Just try it, and you will be amazed.

—

RUNNING

Time: morning

It is difficult to work with anger directly because it may be deeply repressed; so work indirectly. Running will help much anger and fear to evaporate. When you are running for a long time, and breathing deeply, the mind stops functioning and the body takes over.

Step 1:
Start running in the morning on the road. Start with half a mile and then one mile and eventually come to at least three miles. While running use the whole body. Don't run as if you are in a straitjacket, run like a small child using the whole body – hands and feet – and breathe deeply, from the belly.

Step 2:
Then sit under a tree, rest, perspire, and let the cool

breeze come; feel peaceful. You are simply a throbbing body, an alive body, an organism in tune with the whole – just like an animal.

The musculature has to be relaxed. If you like swimming, go swimming also – that will help. But that too has to be done as totally as possible. Anything in which you can become totally involved will be helpful. It is not a question of anger or any other emotion; the question is to get into anything totally. Then you will be able to get into anger and love too. One who knows how to get into anything totally can get into everything totally.

—

BOILING POINT

When: Every day, whenever is a good time for you
Duration: 15 minutes
Need: Alarm clock

Step 1:
Close your room, set the alarm for 15 minutes and become angry – but don't release it. Go on forcing it,

go almost crazy with anger, but don't release it, no expression – not even a pillow to hit. Repress it in every way – the exact opposite of catharsis.

If you feel tension rising in the stomach as if something is going to explode, pull the stomach in; make it as tense as you can. If you feel the shoulders are becoming tense, make them more tense. Let the whole body be as tense as possible, almost as if on a volcano – boiling within and with no release. That is the point to remember – no release, no expression. Don't scream, otherwise the stomach will relax; don't hit anything, otherwise the shoulders will be released of tension. Get heated up as if at 100 degrees, work to a climax.

Step 2:
When the alarm starts going off, try the hardest you can. And as the alarm stops, sit silently, close your eyes, and just watch what is happening. Relax the body.

This heating of the system will force your patterns to melt.

—

OSHO DYNAMIC MEDITATION

Energy can be converted and used. And then, using it, you will be more vital, more alive. The opposite has to be absorbed, then the process becomes dialectical. Effortlessness means not doing anything, inactivity. Effort means doing much, activity. Both have to be there. Do much, but don't be a doer – then you achieve both. Move in the world, but don't be a part of it. Live in the world, but don't let the world live in you. Then the contradiction has been absorbed. Then you are not rejecting anything, not denying anything. Then the whole existence has been accepted.

And that's what I'm doing – Dynamic Meditation is a contradiction. Dynamic means effort, much effort, absolute effort. And meditation means silence, no effort, no activity.

You can call it a dialectical meditation.

Note: You can do this meditation alone, but to start with it can be helpful to do it with other people. It is an individual experience, so remain oblivious of others around you. Wear loose, comfortable clothing.

This meditation is to be done with its specific OSHO Dynamic Meditation music, which has been composed under Osho's direction and which indicates and energetically supports the different stages.

The music is available as a CD and for downloading from a variety of sources listed on osho.com/shop. Also a DVD exists which might be helpful. You can also participate in this meditation in a virtual meditation space by visiting imeditate.osho.com. You will find more information about OSHO® Meditations and the OSHO® Active Meditations™, as well as audio and video instructions and a section on frequently asked questions about meditation at:
www.osho.com/meditation

Instructions:
This is a meditation in which you have to be continuously alert, conscious, aware, whatsoever you do. Remain a witness. And when – in the fourth stage – you have become completely inactive, frozen, then this alertness will come to its peak.

First stage: 10 minutes
Breathing chaotically through the nose, let breathing be intense, deep, fast, without rhythm, with no pattern – and concentrating always on the exhalation. The body will take care of the inhalation. The breath should move deeply into the lungs. Do this as fast

and as hard as you possibly can until you literally become the breathing. Use your natural body movements to help you to build up your energy. Feel it building up, but don't let go during the first stage.

Second stage: 10 minutes
EXPLODE!…
Let go of everything that needs to be thrown out. Follow your body. Give your body freedom to express whatever is there. Go totally mad! Scream, shout, cry, jump, kick, shake, dance, sing, laugh; throw yourself around. Hold nothing back; keep your whole body moving. A little acting often helps to get you started. Never allow your mind to interfere with what is happening. Consciously go mad. Be total.

Third stage: 10 minutes
With arms raised high above your head, jump up and down shouting the mantra, "HOO! HOO! HOO!" as deeply as possible. Each time you land, on the flats of your feet, let the sound hammer deep into the sex center. Give all you have, exhaust yourself completely.

Fourth stage: 15 minutes
STOP! Freeze wherever you are, in whatever position

you find yourself. Don't arrange the body in any way. A cough, a movement, anything will dissipate the energy flow and the effort will be lost. Be a witness to everything that is happening to you.

Fifth stage: 15 minutes
Celebrate! With music and dance express whatsoever is there. Carry your aliveness with you throughout the day.

~

Transformation of Jealousy

A MEDITATION FOR COUPLES

When: At night
Duration: 30 minutes

Step 1: 10 minutes
Sit facing each other, holding each other's hands crosswise.
Look into each other's eyes, as deeply as possible. If the body starts moving and swaying – as it will do – allow it. You can blink, but go on looking into each other's eyes. Don't let go of each other's hands whatever happens. That should not be forgotten.

Step 2: 10 minutes
Both close your eyes and allow the swaying to continue. Just feel that the energy is possessing you.

Step 3: 10 minutes
Now stand and with open eyes sway together, holding hands.
It will almost become a dance – but go on holding hands in the same way.

Do this every night for ten days and then if you feel good, you can repeat it in the morning also – but not more often than twice a day.

This will mix your energies deeply.

—

NOURISHING THE ENERGY OF LOVE

Step 1:
Take a rock in your hand with deep love, with a deep concern. Close your eyes and feel tremendous love for the rock – grateful that it exists, grateful that it accepts your love. Suddenly you will see a pulsation and the energy moving.

Step 2:
By and by there is no need to have an object – just the idea that you love somebody…and energy will start flowing.

Step 3:
Now even the idea can be dropped. Just be loving and energy will be flowing. Love is flow, and whenever we are frozen it is because we don't love.

Love is warmth, and the frozenness cannot happen if the warmth is there. When love is not there everything is cold. You start falling below zero point. So one of the very important things to remember: love is warm. So is hate. Indifference is cold. So sometimes even when you hate, energy starts flowing. Of course that flow is destructive. In anger energy starts flowing – that's why people feel somehow good afterwards: something was released. It is very destructive. It could have been creative if it had been released through love, but it is better than not being released. If you are indifferent you don't flow.

So anything that melts you and warms you up is good. The first choice always must be love. If that is not possible, the second choice is anger. And these are the only two choices – the third is not a choice. That is where people already are. That's why you see so many dead people, walking corpses... They are alive only in name's sake – because they are indifferent. They don't look at the trees, they don't look at the moon, they don't look at the clouds, they don't look at the dewdrops, they don't look at the rainbows, they don't listen to the birds. They are insensitive, indifferent. They exist closed inside themselves in a capsule of indifference. They are not yet born – they are still in the womb.

Once you start flowing... You have discovered a very basic law.

~

FACING JEALOUSY

Sit in your room, close the doors, bring your jealousy into focus. Watch it, see it; let it become as strong a flame as possible. Let it become a strong flame, burn with it and see what it is. And don't from the very beginning say that this is ugly, because that very idea that this is ugly will repress it, will not allow it total expression.

No opinions! Just try to see the existential effect of what jealousy is, the existential fact. No interpretations, no ideologies! Forget all the buddhas and teachings. Just let the jealousy be there. Look into it, look deeply into it. Do this with anger, do this with sadness, hatred, possessiveness. And by and by you will see that just by seeing through things you start getting a transcendental feeling that you are just a witness; the identity is broken. The identity is broken only when you encounter something within you.

Transformation of Fear

ENTERING FEAR

When:
Do Step 1 during the day, at a time when your stomach is empty or 2–3 hours after you have eaten; otherwise you may vomit.
Do Step 2 at night, just before going to sleep.

Step 1: 25–45 minutes
Close the door to the room, be naked if possible, or wear loose clothing, and sit cross legged.
Put your hands just 2" below the navel and press there. Then release the pressure. The pressing acts as a trigger. You can stop pressing once things start happening – after 2 minutes or so.

Just by pressing the hara, great fear will arise and your breathing will start becoming chaotic, so allow it and go into it. You may start feeling a great trembling – cooperate with it. You may feel like rolling around on the ground – roll. If breathing becomes chaotic, allow it; if the hands start moving.... Whatever happens – if you feel like dancing, dance.

Don't manage it, allow it: be possessed. This may last 25–45 minutes, and it will be tremendously beneficial. It may take at least 2 months to complete it, but it will be a Primal, and you will reach a very deep space within yourself.

Step 2: 2–3 minutes
And the second thing, before going to sleep, lie on the bed with eyes closed and imagine a blackboard – as black as you can imagine. Visualize on the board the figure 3, three times. First see it, then erase it; see it, erase it and so on. Then visualize the figure 2 three times, and erase. Then the figure 1, three times and erase; then zero. By the time you reach the third zero, you will feel a great silence unlike you have ever felt before – and that silence will increase as your Primal grows. Try to complete this before you fall asleep. Go slowly, lovingly – it may take 2–3 minutes. There are also these layers inside you, so by the time you come to the zero, you touch the zero layer inside you. The day the primal is complete you will fall into absolute silence – as if the whole existence has suddenly disappeared, nothing is. That will be a great glimpse.

FROM FEAR TO LOVE

Duration: 40–60 minutes

Step 1:
Sit comfortably, with your right hand placed under-neath the left, and thumbs joining. This puts the energy in a certain relationship, a certain posture. The left hand is connected with the right brain and vice versa. The left side is the seat of reason, a coward. A person can't be both an intellectual and brave. The right brain is intuitive.

Step 2:
Relax, close your eyes. let your lower jaw relax so you start breathing through your mouth. Simply sit in this posture, breathing through the mouth. When you breathe through the mouth and not the nose, you establish a new breathing pattern, and thus the old pattern can be broken. Also when you breathe through the nostrils you constantly stimulate the brain. The nose is dual, the mouth is nondual. So when you breathe through the mouth you don't stimulate the brain – the breath goes directly to the chest. It will create a very silent, non dual, new state

of relaxation, and your energies will start flowing in a new way.

~

RELIVING CHILDHOOD

Nothing has to be feared, it has only to be understood. The whole of one's life has to become just a story of understanding – no fear, no anger, nothing is needed. They are unnecessary hindrances to understanding.

PART 1
When: Every night before sleeping
Duration: 10–15 minutes

Step 1:
Sit in your bed with the light off. Become a small child, as small as you can conceive, as you can recall – maybe three years old, beyond that we have almost completely forgotten. All is darkness, you are a small child and you are alone.

Step 2:
Start crying, sway, do gibberish, any sounds, any

nonsense words. Anything goes: sway, cry, weep, laugh; be crazy and let things come. Many sounds will start surfacing. If shouting comes, shout – unaddressed, just for the sheer fun of it.

Do this for 10–15 minutes.

Step 3:

Now go to sleep with that childlike simplicity and innocence.

PART 2

When: In the daytime whenever there is a chance.

Run on the beach like a child, start collecting seashells, colored stones. Or if you are in the garden become a child again; start running after butterflies. Forget your age – play with the birds or with the animals. And whenever you can find children, mix with them, don't remain an adult. Whenever it is possible be naked – and lie on the earth so you can feel like a child again. Make faces at yourself in a mirror; splash in your tub like a child – have plastic ducks to play with; you can find a thousand and one things.

All that is needed is to connect yourself with your

childhood again and then the fear will disappear, because it started there and you have to catch it back in the moment when it started. You have to go back in time, in your memories. You have to go to the root because things can only be changed if we catch hold of their roots... The whole point is to start reliving your childhood. And this will be gone, and when it is gone you will feel real flowering.

—

GROUNDING

It is one of the most prevalent problems for the modern man; the whole of humanity is suffering from uprootedness. When you become aware of it, you will always feel a wavering in the legs, uncertainty, because the legs are really the roots of man. Through his legs man is rooted in the earth. Once you understand a problem directly, it is already on the way to being solved. Now you have to do two or three things…

When: Every morning

Step 1: To be done at the same location as Step 2.

Stand on your feet, just 6–8" apart, and close your eyes. Then first put your whole weight on the right foot, as if you are standing only on the right; the left is unburdened. Feel it – and then shift to the left foot. Have the whole weight on the left foot and relieve the right foot completely, as if it has nothing to do. It is just there on the ground but it has no weight to it. Do this 4–5 times – feeling this shift of energy – and feel how it feels. Then try to be just in the middle, neither on the left nor the right, or on both. Just in the middle – no emphasis, fifty-fifty. That 50–50 feeling will give you more rootedness in the earth.

Step 2:
If you are near the sea, run on the beach, on the sand. If you are not near the sea, run anywhere barefoot – no shoes on, just on the naked earth – let there be a contact between your feet and the earth.

Step 3:
To end with, after you have run, repeat Step 1.

Within a few weeks you will start feeling a great energy and strength in your legs.

And lastly:

Start taking deeper breaths. With shallow breathing one will feel uprooted. The breath must go to the very root of your being, and the root is your sex center. Man is born out of sex. Our energy is sexual. Breathing should go and make contact with your sex energy so there is a continuous massage of the sex center by the breathing. Then you feel rooted. Otherwise if your breathing is shallow and never goes to the sex center there is a gap – which makes you feel wavering, confused, uncertain, not knowing who you are, where you are going, not knowing what your purpose is, why you exist…just drifting. Then you will become lusterless, no life, because how can life be when there is no purpose? And how can there be purpose when you are not rooted in your own energy?

So first: grounding in the earth – which is the mother of all. Then grounding in the sex center – which is the father of all. Then you will be completely at ease, tranquil, collected, centered, grounded.

CHAPTER 8

epilogue

Meditation creates the catalytic agent:
a totally silent mind with no thoughts,
a totally relaxed body with no tensions,
a totally empty heart with no moods,
no feelings, no sentiments,
no emotions.
And then, simply wait.
In this silence, serenity,
just wait...
And out of nowhere
something explodes in you.
Yes, it is an explosion –
of light, of love,
of tremendous bliss,
which remains with you forever.

〜

about Osho

Osho's unique contribution to the understanding of who we are defies categorization. Mystic and scientist, a rebellious spirit whose sole interest is to alert humanity to the urgent need to discover a new way of living. To continue as before is to invite threats to our very survival on this unique and beautiful planet.

His essential point is that only by changing ourselves, one individual at a time, can the outcome of all our "selves" – our societies, our cultures, our beliefs, our world – also change. The doorway to that change is meditation.

Osho the scientist has experimented and scrutinized all the approaches of the past and examined their effects on the modern human being and responded to their shortcomings by creating a new starting point for the hyperactive 21st Century mind: OSHO Active Meditations.

Once the agitation of a modern lifetime has started to settle, "activity" can melt into "passivity," a key starting point of real meditation. To support this next step, Osho has transformed the ancient "art of listening" into a subtle contemporary methodology: the OSHO Talks. Here words become music, the listener discovers who is listening, and the awareness moves from what is being heard to the individual doing the listening. Magically, as silence arises, what needs to be heard is understood directly, free from the distraction of a mind that can only interrupt and interfere with this delicate process.

These thousands of talks cover everything from the individual quest for meaning to the most urgent social and political issues facing society today. Osho's books are not written but are transcribed from audio and video recordings of these extemporaneous talks to international audiences. As he puts it, "So remember: whatever I am saying is not just for you...I am talking also for the future generations."

Osho has been described by *The Sunday Times* in London as one of the "1000 Makers of the 20th Century" and by American author Tom Robbins as "the most dangerous man since Jesus Christ." *Sunday Mid-Day* (India) has selected Osho as one of ten people – along with Gandhi, Nehru and Buddha – who have changed the destiny of India.

About his own work Osho has said that he is helping to create the conditions for the birth of a new kind of human being. He often characterizes this new human being as "Zorba the Buddha" – capable both of enjoying the earthy pleasures of a Zorba the Greek and the silent serenity of a Gautama the Buddha.

Running like a thread through all aspects of Osho's talks and meditations is a vision that encompasses both the timeless wisdom of all ages past and the highest potential of today's (and tomorrow's) science and technology.

Osho is known for his revolutionary contribution to the science of inner transformation, with an approach to meditation that acknowledges the accelerated pace of contemporary life. His unique OSHO Active Meditations™ are designed to first release the accumulated stresses of body and mind, so that it is then easier to take an experience of stillness and thought-free relaxation into daily life.

Two autobiographical works by the author are available:
Autobiography of a Spiritually Incorrect Mystic,
St Martins Press, New York (book and eBook)
Glimpses of a Golden Childhood,
OSHO Media International, Pune, India

OSHO international meditation resort

Each year the Meditation Resort welcomes thousands of people from more than 100 countries. The unique campus provides an opportunity for a direct personal experience of a new way of living – with more aware-ness, relaxation, celebration and creativity. A great variety of around-the-clock and around-the-year pro-gram options are available. Doing nothing and just relaxing is one of them!

All of the programs are based on Osho's vision of "Zorba the Buddha" – a qualitatively new kind of human being who is able *both* to participate cre-atively in everyday life *and* to relax into silence and meditation.

Location
Located 100 miles southeast of Mumbai in the thriving modern city of Pune, India, the OSHO International Meditation Resort is a holiday destina-tion with a difference. The Meditation Resort is spread over 28 acres of spectacular gardens in a beautiful tree-lined residential area.

OSHO Meditations
A full daily schedule of meditations for every type

of person includes both traditional and revolutionary methods, and particularly the OSHO Active Meditations™. The daily meditation program takes place in what must be the world's largest meditation hall, the OSHO Auditorium.

OSHO Multiversity
Individual sessions, courses and workshops cover everything from creative arts to holistic health, personal transformation, relationship and life transition, transforming meditation into a lifestyle for life and work, esoteric sciences, and the "Zen" approach to sports and recreation. The secret of the OSHO Multiversity's success lies in the fact that all its programs are combined with meditation, supporting the understanding that as human beings we are far more than the sum of our parts.

OSHO Basho Spa
The luxurious Basho Spa provides for leisurely open-air swimming surrounded by trees and tropical green. The uniquely styled, spacious Jacuzzi, the saunas, gym, tennis courts...all these are enhanced by their stunningly beautiful setting.

Cuisine
A variety of different eating areas serve delicious Western, Asian and Indian vegetarian food – most of it organically grown especially for the Meditation

Resort. Breads and cakes are baked in the resort's own bakery.

Night life
There are many evening events to choose from – dancing being at the top of the list! Other activities include full-moon meditations beneath the stars, variety shows, music performances and meditations for daily life.

Facilities
You can buy all of your basic necessities and toiletries in the Galleria. The Multimedia Gallery sells a large range of OSHO media products. There is also a bank, a travel agency and a Cyber Café on-campus. For those who enjoy shopping, Pune provides all the options, ranging from traditional and ethnic Indian products to all of the global brand-name stores.

Accommodation
You can choose to stay in the elegant rooms of the OSHO Guest-house, or for longer stays on campus you can select one of the OSHO Living-In programs. Additionally there is a plentiful variety of nearby hotels and serviced apartments.

www.osho.com/meditationresort
www.osho.com/guesthouse
www.osho.com/livingin

more books and eBooks by OSHO media international

The God Conspiracy:
The Path from Superstition to Super Consciousness

Discover the Buddha: 53 Meditations to Meet the Buddha Within
Gold Nuggets: Messages from Existence

<u>OSHO Classics</u>
The Book of Wisdom: The Heart of Tibetan Buddhism.
The Mustard Seed: The Revolutionary Teachings of Jesus
Ancient Music in the Pines: In Zen, Mind Suddenly Stops
The Empty Boat: Encounters with Nothingness
A Bird on the Wing: Zen Anecdotes for Everyday Life
The Path of Yoga: Discovering the Essence and Origin of Yoga
And the Flowers Showered: The Freudian Couch and Zen

Nirvana: The Last Nightmare: Learning to Trust in Life

The Goose Is Out: Zen in Action

Absolute Tao: Subtle Is the Way to Love, Happiness and Truth

The Tantra Experience: Evolution through Love

Tantric Transformation: When Love Meets Meditation

Pillars of Consciousness (illustrated)

BUDDHA: His Life and Teachings and Impact on Humanity

ZEN: Its History and Teachings and Impact on Humanity

TANTRA: The Way of Acceptance

TAO: The State and the Art

Authentic Living

Danger: Truth at Work: The Courage to Accept the Unknowable

The Magic of Self-Respect: Awakening to Your Own Awareness
Born With a Question Mark in Your Heart

<u>OSHO eBooks and "OSHO-Singles"</u>
Emotions: Freedom from Anger, Jealousy and Fear
Meditation: The First and Last Freedom
What Is Meditation?
The Book of Secrets: 112 Meditations to Discover the Mystery Within

20 Difficult Things to Accomplish in This World
Compassion, Love and Sex
Hypnosis in the Service of Meditation
Why Is Communication So Difficult, Particularly between Lovers?
Bringing Up Children
Why Should I Grieve Now?: facing a loss and letting it go
Love and Hate: just two sides of the same coin

Next Time You Feel Angry...
Next Time You Feel Lonely...
Next Time You Feel Suicidal...

<u>OSHO Media BLOG</u>
http://oshomedia.blog.osho.com

for more information

www. **OSHO** .com

a comprehensive multi-language website including a magazine, OSHO Books, OSHO Talks in audio and video formats, the OSHO Library text archive in English and Hindi and extensive information about OSHO Meditations. You will also find the program schedule of the OSHO Multiversity and information about the OSHO International Meditation Resort.

http://OSHO.com/AllAboutOSHO
http://OSHO.com/Resort
http://OSHO.com/Shop
http://www.youtube.com/OSHO
http://www.Twitter.com/OSHO
http://www.facebook.com/pages/OSHO.International

To contact OSHO International Foundation:
www.osho.com/oshointernational,
oshointernational@oshointernational.com